Soccer
RULES

Soccer

RULES

KEN GOLDMAN

BLANDFORD

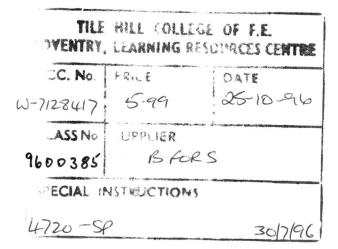
A BLANDFORD BOOK

First published in the UK by Blandford
A Cassell Imprint
Cassell Plc, Wellington House,
125 Strand, London WC2R 0BB

Distributed in the United States by
Sterling Publishing Co., Inc.
387 Park Avenue South, New York,
NY 10016-8810

Distributed in Australia by Capricorn Link
(Australia) Pty Ltd
2/13 Carrington Road, Castle Hill, NSW 2154

British Library Cataloguing-in-Publication Data
A catalogue entry for this title is available from
the British Library

ISBN 0-7137-2474-9

Typeset by Litho Link Ltd, Welshpool, Powys,
Wales

Printed and bound in Great Britain by The Bath
Press, Avon

ACKNOWLEDGEMENTS

The author and publishers would like to thank
Colorsport for supplying the photographs
reproduced in this book.

Cover Jürgen Klinsmann and Ronald
Koeman, two of the leading players in
European club soccer, clash when playing for
their countries, Germany and Holland. The
Dutchman's foot seems high but he is looking
at the ball and clearly trying to play it.

Frontispiece A high catch by the keeper in a
crowded penalty area requires the vigilant
referee to be watching for him being impeded
by members of the attacking side; he must be
sure, however, that it is not his own defenders
which hinder him. This is Gary Walsh in action
for Manchester United against Ipswich.

CONTENTS

INTRODUCTION

At the start of the nineteenth century football began to take on a shape that made it a cross between today's modern soccer and rugby. With the growth of education, particularly at public schools, and a rise in social awareness it was felt that games should be played to improve health and to promote a competitive spirit which would be useful in post-school life. The most serious advances took place at Rugby School. There Dr Thomas Arnold was so interested in its potential that he organized football in such a way as to apply a set of principles and restrictions to the game.

For football to achieve any real mass popularity and progress it was realized that there had to be a set of rules to govern the way it was played. At Cambridge University in 1848 a seven-hour meeting took place between 40 men who represented different public schools; the result was the 'Cambridge Rules'. Another meeting at the same venue in 1862 saw further modification to these Rules.

The most momentous date in the history of the laws of soccer is Monday 26 October 1863, when there was a meeting between the captains and other representatives of football clubs in the London area. Its purpose was to adopt a set of Rules that all football players nationally should adhere to and whose principles should be carried into effect as quickly as practicable. The resolution was passed 'that it was advisable that a Football Association should be formed for the purpose of setting a code of Rules for the regulation of the game of football'.

By 1877 free kicks and throw-ins were adopted in the modern style and a permanent crossbar was introduced. Duration of the match was limited to 90 minutes, handling the ball was restricted to goalkeepers and it was specified that neutral referees were to be appointed. The chronological order of other variations consisted of the restriction of the number of players to 11 in 1870 and the introduction of the goal kick in 1869 and the corner kick in 1872, with the penalty kick following in 1891.

The twentieth century's most fundamental change to the game occurred at the start of the 1925/26 season. Because cleverly organized defences were able to move up the field when opponents attacked in order to put those opponents offside, the game lost much of its sparkle for players and spectators alike. For this reason the current Law was adopted whereby in order for the attacking side to be ruled offside the number of opponents required to be between the attacker and the goal line was reduced from three to two.

As the result of continual changes it was felt that the Rules should be recodified into 'Laws of the Game', and under the guidance of Stanley Rous this took place by the end of 1938.

In 1886 an International Board was established which was responsible for reviewing and if necessary amending the Laws of the Game. It comprised representatives from each of the four 'home' countries of England, Ireland, Scotland and Wales. A separate organization, the Fédération Internationale de Football Association (FIFA), was set up in 1904 by Belgium, Denmark, France, Netherlands, Spain, Sweden and Switzerland, eventually to be joined by the four home countries.

Since the recodification of the game very little has changed in the 17 Laws themselves although the International Board has made a number of changes designed to speed up the game in order to improve it as a spectacle and to stop 'gamesmanship'. With the growth of competitive football there has been a need to decide cup competitions within a reasonable time, so the 'penalty decider' has been introduced. As we shall see later, the most recent variations have been to the interpretation of the offside law with the intention of encouraging attacking play.

● **NOTE**

Throughout the book, players and officials are referred to as 'he'. This is done purely for grammatical convenience, and is in no way intended to exclude women.

CONVERSION TABLE OF MEASUREMENTS
FOR THE LAWS OF THE GAME

130 yd – 120 m	8 ft – 2.44 m
120 yd – 110 m	5 ft – 1.50 m
110 yd – 100 m	28 in – 0.71 m
100 yd – 90 m	27 in – 0.68 m
80 yd – 75 m	9 in – 0.22 m
70 yd – 64 m	5 in – 0.12 m
50 yd – 45 m	½ in – 12.7 mm
18 yd – 16.50 m	⅜ in – 10 mm
12 yd – 11 m	14 oz – 396 g
10 yd – 9.15 m	16 oz – 453 g
8 yd – 7.32 m	8.5 lb/sq in – 600 g/cm^2
6 yd – 5.50 m	15.6 lb/sq in – 1,100 g/cm^2
1 yd – 1 m	

LONGITUDE AND LATITUDE

● THE PITCH, ITS MARKINGS AND THE 'FOOTBALL FURNITURE'

In the game's history it took a long time for Laws to be devised which governed and controlled the confines of the pitch (to avoid the game becoming unruly and spreading for uncontrollable distances). That development saw goals being erected and painted markings on the pitch laid down to define relevant areas.

Football is now played on a pitch the playing surface of which can be either grass or other artificial surfaces, including artificial turf, shale, 'red grass' or mud, but FIFA has indicated that for the World Cup and other competitive international matches grass must be used as the playing surface. The pitch and its dimensions are governed by Law 1 under the heading 'Field of Play'.

The field itself must measure between 100 and 130 yds in length and be 50 to 100 yds wide (Figure 1). Under no circumstances can the pitch be square; it must always be rectangular with the length exceeding the width. There are more stringent restrictions for international matches, the International Board specifying maximum dimensions of 120 yds × 82 yds and minimum ones of 109 yds × 70 yds.

The boundary lines drawn down the long side of the pitch are called touchlines and those across the width of the pitch at each end are goal lines. Sometimes the goal line is referred to by a similar rugby term, 'byline', but this is not official terminology. All boundary lines and similar pitch markings are 5 in. wide and form part of the field of play.

The other pitch markings are as follows. A centre line is drawn across

Fig 1   The pitch and its markings

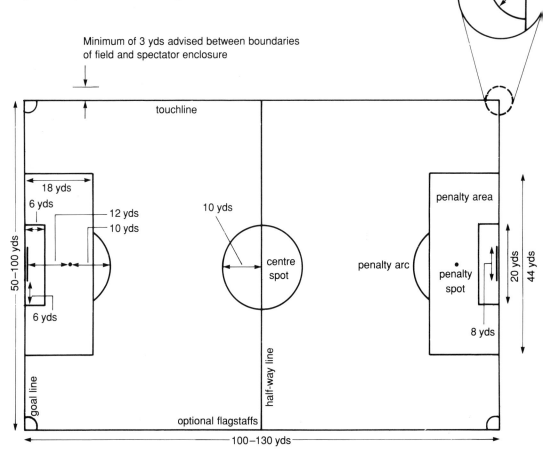

Minimum of 3 yds advised between boundaries
of field and spectator enclosure

the pitch at a point midway between the two touchlines. At the middle of the centre line is a centre spot where all kick-offs (as later mentioned) start from. A circle with a 10 yd radius is drawn from the centre spot and is known as the centre circle. At each corner of the field of play are four corner posts each with a minimum height of 5 ft, the minimum height being to protect players from injury. Each post must have a non-pointed top, and must have a flag on top. The corner posts are positioned at the points where the goal lines and touchlines meet (Figure 2). A quadrant with a 1 yd radius is drawn at each corner of the field. As an additional option, similar flag-posts may be placed 1 yd outside the touchline opposite the centre line, which is usually referred to as the 'half-way line' (Figure 2A).

All dimensions on the field of play

must be marked with distinctive lines, not be cut out with V-shaped ruts.

At the centre of each goal line is a goal. Each goal consists of two uprights placed 8 yds apart (this is the inside measurement between the two posts) and joined at the top by a crossbar 8 ft (to the lower part of the bar) above the ground (Figure 3). The uprights and crossbars should not exceed 5 in. in width and should all be of the same width. Both the goal posts and crossbars must be made of wood or metal or other approved material. There are a number of permissible variations to their shape: they may be square, rectangular, round, half round or elliptical. It is particularly emphasized that the goal posts must be white, but there is seemingly nothing to stop the crossbar being painted another colour, or being striped.

Nets are normally fitted to the back of the uprights and crossbar, in order to help make it clear when a goal has been scored. In matches where there are no nets, disputes often arise as to whether the ball has crossed the goal line inside or outside the goal.

In a competitive match, if the crossbar becomes displaced or broken play has to be stopped and if it cannot be replaced or repaired the match has to be abandoned. As mentioned in the Introduction, originally there was no crossbar, a rope being considered satisfactory, whereas nowadays it is clearly decreed that a rope is not a satisfactory substitute for a crossbar except in a friendly match, where by mutual consent play may be resumed either without a crossbar or with the use of a rope. However, in those circumstances the players must accept that if the ball crosses the goal line at a point at which the referee believes a goal would have been scored had there been a crossbar, he is entitled to award a goal.

The goals themselves at each end are bounded by a 'goal area'. Two lines are drawn at right angles to the goal line 6 yds from each goal post. They extend into the field of play for a distance of 6 yds and are joined by a

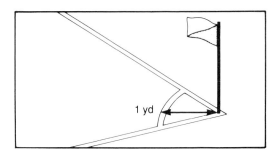

Fig 2   The corner flag (compulsory)

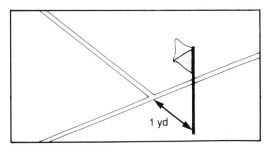

Fig 2A   The halfway flag (optional)

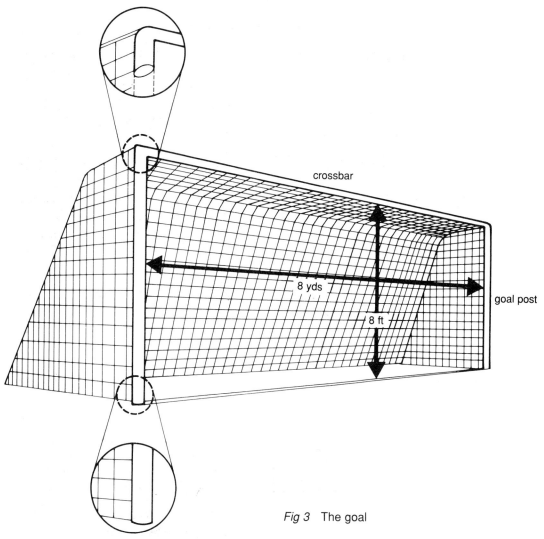

Fig 3 The goal

line parallel to the goal line (Figure 4). The goal area forms part of a larger area known as the penalty area. This is created by drawing two lines at right angles to the goal line 18 yds from each goal post and extending into the field of play a distance of 18 yds. They are also joined by a line parallel to the goal line (Figure 5).

When a serious offence of a deliberate nature occurs in the penalty area the referee ordinarily awards a penalty kick, usually called a 'penalty'. The penalty is taken from a penalty spot, which is marked 12 yds from the goal line and facing the midpoint of the goal. It is actually measured along an undrawn line at right angles thereto.

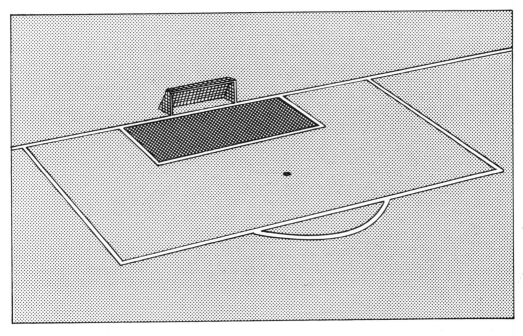

Fig 4   The goal area

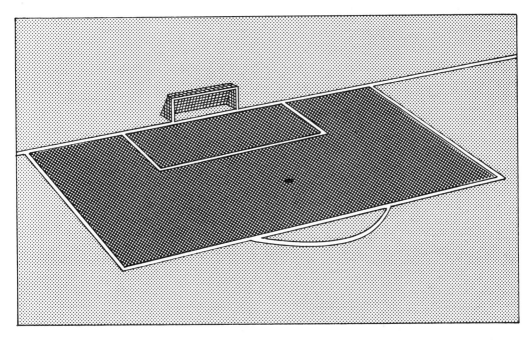

Fig 5   The penalty area

In order to ensure that the penalty complies with the Laws, which state that defenders have to be 10 yds from the ball when a penalty kick is taken, all players must stand 10 yds outside the penalty area and behind the penalty mark. Ten yards from the penalty spot an arc with a radius of 10 yds is drawn outside the penalty area, and forms an addition to the area that players must be outside.

No markings other than the official markings mentioned here may be used. However, in order further to protect players a line may be marked behind the goal lines at least 7 ft from the corner flags going through to a point situated at least 11 ft 6 in. behind the intersection of the goal line with the line marking the goal area, to a point situated at least 20 ft behind the goal posts which may be known as a 'photographers' line', no photographer being allowed to pass over that line under any circumstances. Recently the International Board has sanctioned a further area known as a 'technical area' which relates to matches played in stadiums with a designated place for technical staff and substitutes. This technical area is considered to extend 3 ft on either side of the designated seating area and extends forward up to a distance of 3 ft

away from the touchlines. Markings are not required, but are recommended, to define the area and the number of persons permitted to occupy that area is defined by the rules of the competition.

Further lines (which are totally unofficial) 11 yds from the corner flags, and at right angles to the goal lines, are helpful in showing the distance beyond which players must not encroach, for example when a corner kick is taken, they must not join the official boundary lines. If they do, or if a groundsman marks out a line in the middle of the goal area to assist the goalkeeper in working out his positioning, the referee must not commence the game until such lines are removed and he is required to report these infractions to the relevant governing body in charge of the competition.

All publicity is forbidden both on the field and on the 'football furniture'.

Previous pages John Barnes strikes a free kick for Liverpool in a match against Dinamo Kiev. The defensive wall must be 10 yds away from the ball but can consist of any number of players.

THE BALL

Football, as the name suggests, involves using the feet to propel a round object with the aim of scoring a goal. Originally the ball was made of wicker, and over the years a number of items have been utilized, including in informal matches, rags and oranges. However, when the Laws were codified it was decided that one particular Law, now Law 2, should prescribe requirements for the ball. For much of organized football prior to the mid-1950s the football consisted of a leather case with a rubber bladder inside which was pumped up to give the ball the prescribed size and weight. Normally such balls were dun (brownish-grey) in colour but occasionally when a match was played on snow they were painted orange or red so they could be seen on the white surface. However, with the advent of floodlit football it became necessary in order to see the ball for it to be painted white. Unfortunately the old type of ball, which had to be kept in condition and shape by the use of dubbin, tended during the course of a game to pick up and retain water in wet conditions, so for this reason too it became usual for the ball to be coated in white plastic. As technology has advanced, leather has often given way to synthetic materials and the bladder inside it has become obsolete.

So far as the Law is concerned the ball has to be spherical and nowadays the outer casing must be of leather or any other material which is approved by the International Board. Obviously anything which may prove dangerous or harmful to the players must not be used.

The circumference of the ball cannot be more than 28 in. or less than 27 in. (Figure 6) and at the start of the game (old-style balls were not abandoned during the match when they picked up water) it must weigh not more than 16 oz. nor less than 14 oz. The pressure of the ball is specified by a complex formula; it is measured at sea level

Fig 6
The ball

27–28 in.

and there have been interesting variations in the movement of the ball in the air at altitude. However, if the ball bursts or becomes deflated during the course of the match the referee obtains a new ball (as he would do if an old ball were lost). The game is then restarted by means of a dropped ball, the ball being dropped at the place where the ball became impaired unless that place was within the goal area, in which case the ball is dropped on the six-yard line of the goal area at the point nearest to where the damage occurred when play was stopped. If a ball is damaged or lost after it passes over one of the boundaries the game is recommenced by the appropriate restart (see pages 42–46).

THE PERFORMERS

● THE TEAMS, THE PLAYERS AND THEIR EQUIPMENT

The evolutionary process in football eventually honed down a large pack of players to 11. However, the number has been varied by the introduction, in the 1960s, of substitutes. A match can now involve as many as 14 players per side, consisting of three substitutes. References to players and teams are contained in Law 3.

Apart from the situation where a player or players are dismissed from the match, football is a sport played by two equal teams of 11 players. Although that number cannot be exceeded, it can be reduced according to the rules of the competition under which it is played. However, the International Board has expressed the view that a match should not be considered valid if there are fewer than seven players in either team. Of the number who take part, one shall at all times be designated as a goalkeeper and wear clothing which distinguishes him. Any player may change places with the goalkeeper, but the referee must be informed before the change takes place and that change must be made during a stoppage in play.

Before the introduction of substitutes that was basically the whole of the Law since everything else connected with players and teams related to their equipment. Since substitutes have been allowed, Law 3 has been extended quite considerably. Initially one substitute was allowed to replace an injured player. The rule was subsequently modified to include substitution for tactical purposes. Then two named substitutes were allowed. Later, a further amendment stated that two substitutes could be used but out of five named. The International Board has now decreed that the rules of the competition shall state how many, if any, substitutes may be designated and how many of those designated may be used. From 1995, a team may now use a third substitute. Some competitions already employed this system but it was thought that the International Board, when the matter was put to it, would disqualify a named substitute goalkeeper if the original goalkeeper was ordered off. However, contrary to expectation, the International Board has now firmly specified that a substitute goalkeeper may subsequently replace the dismissed goalkeeper. It has to be understood that if that situation does occur then an outfield player must leave the field since the purpose of the referee dismissing the original goalkeeper was to reduce the number of players in the offending team. Even in the position of a sending off the referee must be informed of the proposed substitution before it is made. A player may only enter the field on the half-way line when the player he is replacing has left and when he has received a signal from the referee to do so.

The foregoing rules apply to matches under the authority of international associations or national

No sending off is good for a team but to lose your goalkeeper is particularly serious. Here, Peter Schmeichel of Manchester United is dismissed in a cup match but United still managed to win the game.

associations but substitutes may be used in any other match provided the two teams reach prior agreement on the maximum number of substitutes to be used. Two from five in competitive matches (not the World Cup, where presently eleven may be named from whom three may be chosen) can be extended in friendly matches but in this case they must not exceed five and the referee must be notified before the start of the game. Failure either to agree the number or to notify the referee will mean that only three substitutes will be permitted.

Should a player be ordered off before play begins he may be replaced only by one of the named substitutes and the kick-off must not be delayed so that the substitute may join the match. This also applies if a team starts with fewer than 11 men. In those circumstances a player or players may join the match until just before it finishes.

However, should the referee discover that more than 11 players from one team are on the field at the same time, no matter how late in the game it is, he must abandon the match. If there is sufficient time to replay it he must restart it from the beginning. Neither a player nor a named substitute who has been ordered off after play has started may be replaced, unless the ordering off is a temporary one to make the player comply with Law 4, which relates to players' equipment.

There can be no doubt about what is to be worn by players since Law 4 specifies it in detail. It indicates that whatever else may be worn with the referee's permission (which can include such things as track suit trousers, gloves, tights, caps for goalkeepers and cycling shorts under the main shorts) there is a basic compulsory set of equipment, which consists of a jersey or shirt, shorts, socks (still, surprisingly, called stockings) shin guards and footwear.

For many years shin guards were optional and some players would not wear them because they were considered to slow the player down. Others could not afford them and would use such things as paperback books, magazines or even rolled-up newspaper. Thus the use of shin pads to protect the lower leg has always been a contentious issue. However, FIFA, worried about the increasing number of leg injuries and especially the danger from cuts, on medical

advice in the early 1990s decreed that shin pads should be compulsory. They are made of rubber, plastic, polyurethane or similar substances, or any material which is deemed suitable by the International Board and which will afford a reasonable degree of protection. The shin guards must be covered by the socks.

Where cycling shorts or thermo-pants are worn the colour must be predominantly the same colour as the player's shorts. For distinguishing purposes the goalkeeper must wear colours which differentiate him from the other players. It is also important that they differentiate him from the referee, which is particularly necessary now that referees often wear not black but any of a variety of different colours.

No player is allowed to wear anything which is dangerous to another player and so it is essential that jewellery is either removed or, in the case of rings, taped up. A player wearing articles not permitted by the Laws and which constitute a danger to other players will be required by the referee to remove them. If the player refuses to carry out that instruction he cannot take part in the match. Should a player need to replace or obtain any equipment the referee must require the player to leave the field in order to resolve the matter once the ball goes out of play unless by that time the player has already corrected the situation. Any player who goes off the field for the purposes described is only allowed to re-enter the field on the referee's signal.

The Law specifies that players must use footwear and not play with taped or bare feet. However, the Law is now far more vague than it used to be on the question of footwear because it recognizes that different playing surfaces may require different kinds of boots or training shoes. In practice, most players will wear boots with studs or bars in them. The preference is for studs which are made of nylon, rubber, aluminium or leather for wet grounds and moulded studs normally of rubber for hard grounds. A special type of 'ice' stud is used in northern Europe for playing on frozen pitches. Whereas the law used to specify that studs and bars had to be of a minimum width and not pointed it now merely requires that they shall not be dangerous. In International matches the referee is required to inspect the studs of players prior to the commencement of the match. The rules of any competition may also include a similar provision, and indeed if any objection is referred to the referee about the condition of a player's boots the referee may call for an immediate inspection of the same.

HOW THE GAME
IS PLAYED

● ITS START, TIMING AND SCORING PROCEDURES

The following principles encompass Laws 7 to 10 inclusive. When the rule-makers met, they realized that every game needs restrictions otherwise it would cover undefined areas of ground and continue for an indefinite period. It was specified that play should be divided into two equal halves of 45 minutes each, although this can be reduced either by the rules of the competition or by agreement between the two teams. While the game cannot be shortened, except by consent, it can be extended by the referee, who acts as sole timekeeper and must decide on his own discretion the amount of time to be added for such things as assessing injuries to players on the field or moving them off the field; the period of time taken to substitute players; and time wasting or other causes, which can cover a multitude of problems including invasions of the pitch by humans or animals and adverse weather conditions. Time is also added should a penalty kick be about to be taken at or after the expiration of the normal period in either half.

Until recently the half-time interval could not exceed five minutes except with the referee's permission, but has now been limited to 15 minutes under all circumstances. The referee cannot, though, ask the players to forgo the interval as it is their right to have a break. It is also not permissible to have two halves of differing periods with time lost in the first half being made up in the second.

If a game has to last for a specified duration it must have a method of starting and finishing. The finish is, as we have seen, a matter for the referee's sole discretion but the start of play has defined requirements. The first of these is for the two captains to meet with the referee to spin a coin, the winner having the choice either of ends or of kick-off. The winning captain makes the choice for the first half; the teams change ends at the start of the second half. Every time a kick-off occurs the teams are positioned in their respective halves of the field and cannot move until the ball has been kicked into play. It is in play once it has travelled its own circumference in a forward motion at a signal from the referee. The ball has to be stationary on the ground in the centre of the field at every kick-off. The player taking the kick-off may not play the ball again until it has been touched by another player. Furthermore, opponents must be 10 yds from the ball until it has actually been kicked off (Figure 7). The same procedure is adopted after a goal has been scored and to commence the second half, when the two teams will have changed ends. The kick-off then goes to the opposite team to that which originally kicked off since no team may kick off both the first and second halves.

Sometimes in charity matches or carnival events a celebrity is asked to kick off the game. That is not regarded by the Laws as a valid kick-off and once such a celebrity has performed

Fig 7 The kick-off

his or her task the game must be commenced with a legitimate kick-off.

Since scoring goals is the main object of the game it is necessary to define the method by which they are scored. This is encompassed entirely in Law 10, which directs that the ball be propelled by foot or any other part of the body except the hands or arms under the crossbar and between the goal posts with the whole of the ball crossing over the whole of the goal line. It must not be thrown or carried, although if the ball unintentionally strikes the hand or arm of any player and is deflected into the goal it shall count as a legitimate score. Obviously the team scoring the greater number of goals during the match is the winner, but if each side scores the same number of goals or no goals at all are scored, the game is termed a 'draw'. In

Fig 8   In play/out of play

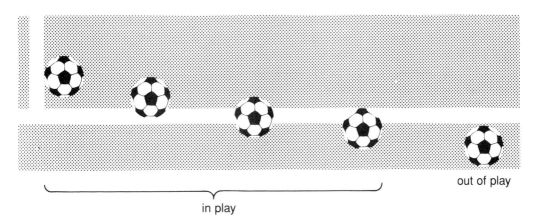

out of play

in play

Fig 8A
Goal/no goal

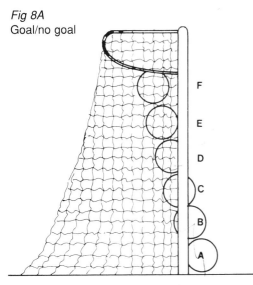

Only balls E and F count as goals

Left   A goal-mouth scramble in a top English match between Queens Park Rangers and Aston Villa. The whole ball must be over the line for a goal to be scored; the linesman must be well positioned at the corner flag in such situations.

cases of drawn games during cup competitions it is the rules of that competition which determine the method by which a winner is decided.

Sometimes outside agencies prevent the ball passing into the goal. This can occur when the ball becomes deflated but other situations can occur such as a spectator interfering with play. In any such case, if it happens during the normal course of play the referee must stop the game and restart it by dropping the ball at the place where it came into contact with the interference – unless it happens to be within the goal area at the time, in which case it is taken back to the goal area line and dropped at the point nearest to where the ball was when play was stopped.

It is important to understand that the whole of the ball has to pass over the whole of the boundaries for there to be some form of restart whether it be a goal, a kick-off, a throw-in, a goal

27

kick or a corner (Figure 8). Thus the ball is out of play when it has crossed the boundary lines whether on the ground or in the air. Additionally, the ball is deemed out of play when the game has been stopped by the referee. At all other times, from the start to the end of the game, the ball is 'in play'. Thus if it strikes the goal posts, crossbar, corner flag or even the referee or a linesman when they are in the field of play the game continues. Players and spectators should of course realize that even if they consider that some form of infringement has taken place the ball continues in play until the referee stops the game and makes a definitive decision.

'OFF AND RUNNING'

● THE OFFSIDE PROVISIONS

On the face of it, Law 11, the offside Law, is one of the shortest of all the governing regulations and therefore one might expect it to be one of the simplest. In practice, it is without doubt the most complicated of all the Laws both to understand and to administer.

The Law states that a player will be deemed to be in an offside position if he is nearer to his opponents' goal line than the ball is. There then follow three basic but vital exceptions. The first is if the player being judged is in his own half of the field. Second, if he is not nearer to his opponents' goal line than at least two of his opponents. Third, the player is not offside if he receives the ball directly from a goal kick, a corner kick or a throw-in. At one stage this list included both a dropped ball and a penalty but these have now been removed.

Although there should be no problems in those aspects of the Law, it is only when a further judgement has to be made that the complications really arise. This is because a player is to be declared offside and penalized when in an offside position only if at the moment the ball has touched or been played by one of his team-mates he is, in the referee's opinion, involved in 'active' play by interfering with play or with an opponent or seeking to gain an advantage by being in that position. Thus it is possible to trespass into an offside position but still not to be offside. It is clearly the intention of the player to become a part of, rather than apart from, the action which counts.

One of the biggest problems in interpretation comes in the difference between the specification in the Law itself and the International Board's ruling as to how it is to be applied. All offside has to be judged not when the player receives the ball but at the moment the ball was last *played*. However, there has been no definition of the word 'play' despite considerable criticism of that omission. The International Board indicates that a player is to be judged not when he receives the ball but at the moment when the ball was *passed* to him by a member of his own side. Therefore a player who is not offside when the ball is passed cannot become offside if he arrives before the ball and then receives it.

In the recent past the emphasis has moved from the defensive mode to the attacking mode and currently an attacking player who is level with his second last opponent or with the last two opponents is not in an offside position. Note that one of those two opponents can be the opposition goalkeeper.

In the 1994 World Cup FIFA required referees to move still further in favour of promoting attacking play. The intention now is that both referees and linesmen will exercise any doubt in favour of the attacking rather than the defending team. They are now also required to consider whether players are in 'active' or 'passive' positions. Those actively taking part will be ruled offside but those who are well away from what could be described as a 'zone of activity' and are neither interfering with play nor seeking to gain an advantage will not be ruled offside. Players who are not offside in a given situation are generally referred to as being 'onside'.

In view of the complexity of this Law it is recommended that the following illustrations be studied carefully.

Diagrams illustrating points in connection with offside

Clear pass to one of the same side

A1 is in possession of the ball and, having A2 in front, passes to him.

A2 becomes offside as he is in front of A1 and there are not at least two opponents between him and the goal line when the ball is passed to him by A1.

Ball rebounding from goal posts or cross-bar

A1 shoots for goal and the ball rebounds from the goal post into play.

A2 nets the rebound.

A2 is offside because the ball is last played by A1, a team-mate, and when A1 played it A2 was in front of the ball and did not have at least two opponents between him and the goal line, and was in an active position.

Ball touching an opponent

A1 shoots at goal. D1 runs from position 1 to position 2 to intercept the ball, but it is deflected to A2, who scores.

A2 is offside as he was in an offside position at the moment the ball was played by one of his own team and in an active position, therefore interfering with play, notwithstanding that the ball was deflected by D1.

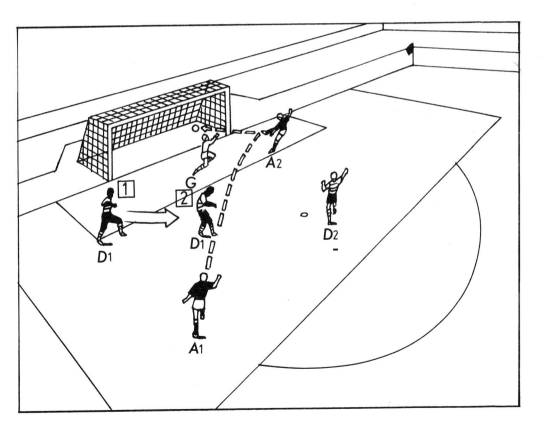

Obstructing the goalkeeper

A1 shoots at goal and scores. A2, however, is obstructing G so that he cannot get to the ball.

The goal must be disallowed, because A2 is in an active offside position and may not touch the ball himself, nor in any way interfere with an opponent.

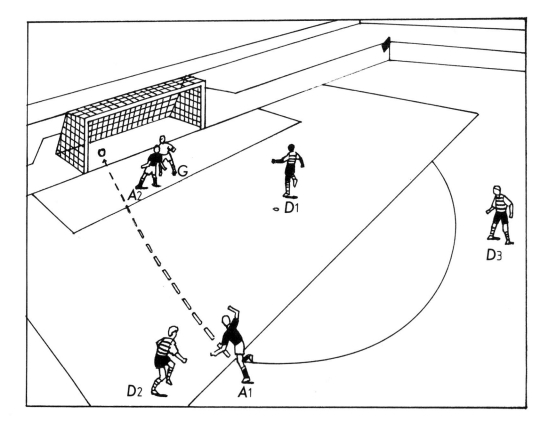

Clear pass to one of the same side

A1 is in possession of the ball and, having D1 in front, passes into the penalty area. A2 runs from position 1 to position 2.

A2 cannot be offside because at the moment the ball was passed by A1 he was not in front of the ball, and he had at least two opponents between him and the goal line.

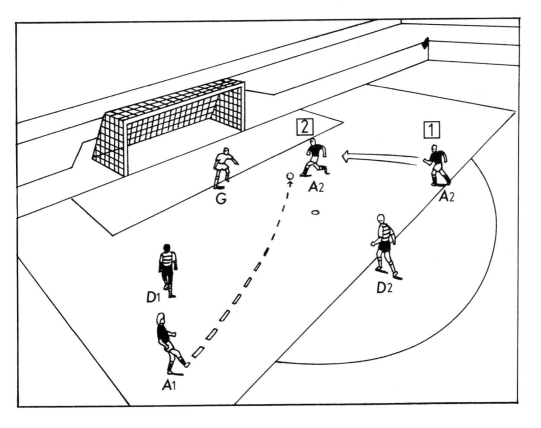

Another clear pass to one of the same side

A1 is in possession of the ball and, having D1 challenging, passes to A2.

A2 cannot be offside because he is level with G and D2 when the ball is passed by A1 and is not nearer his opponents' goal line than at least two defenders.

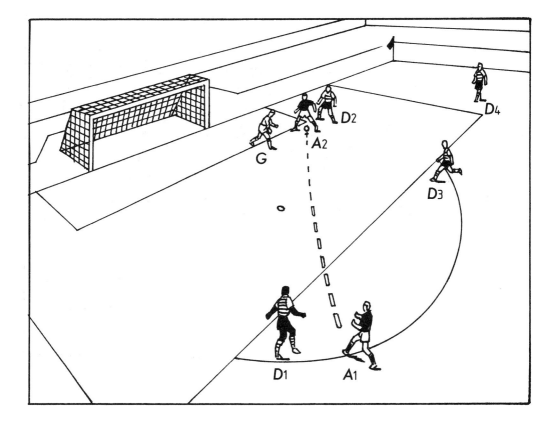

At a corner kick

A1 curls in a corner kick and the ball
goes to A2, who scores.

A2 has only one opponent (namely G)
between him and the goal line, but he
is not offside because a player cannot
be offside from a corner kick.

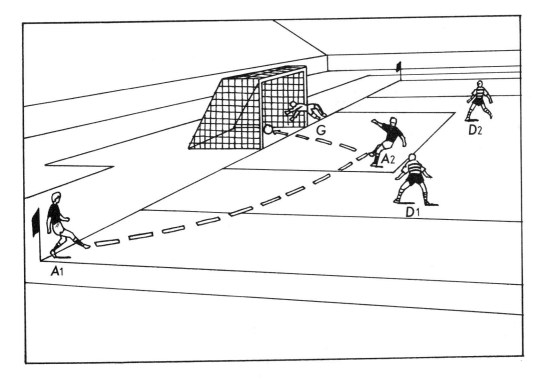

At a throw-in

A1 throws the ball directly to A2.

Although A2 is in front of the ball and there are not at least two opponents between him and the goal line, he is not offside because a player can never be offside from a throw-in.

A player receiving the ball in his own half of the field is not offside when he enters his opponents' half of the field of play

If A2 is in his own half of the field he is onside, although he is in front of the ball and there are not at least two defenders nearer their own goal line when A1 last played the ball. A2 therefore cannot be offside when he enters his opponents' half of the field.

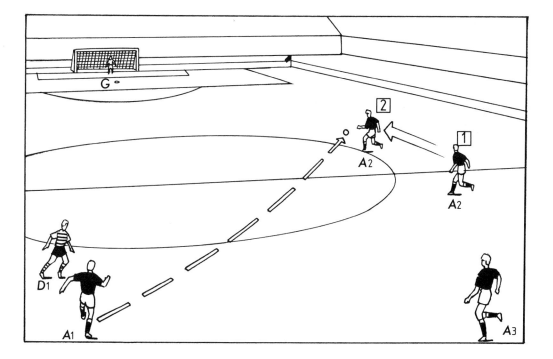

Not offside

Even though A2 is nearer his opponents' goal line than two opponents because A2 is not in a zone of activity he is thus not interfering with the play or an opponent when A1 legitimately scores.

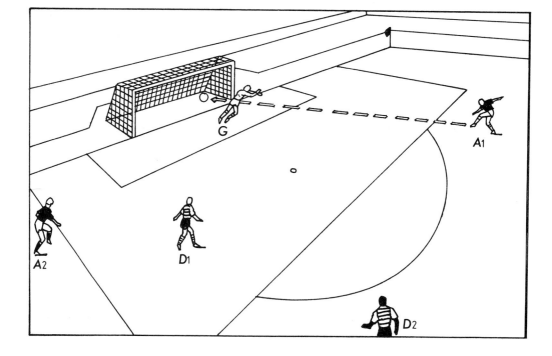

Offside

Even though A2 is out wide he is in an offside position, and also in an active position or zone despite the fact that the shot from A1 is parried by the goalkeeper being the last defender to touch the ball. But A2 cannot run in and score because he is deemed to be in the same 'phase' of active play.

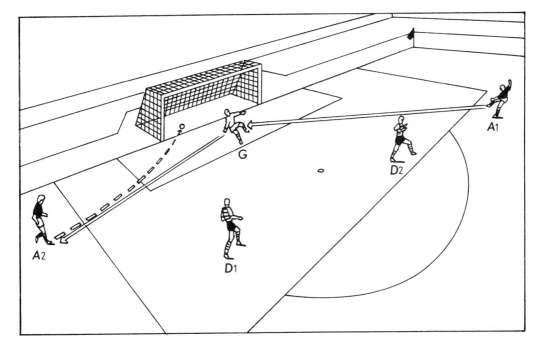

RESTARTS

Apart from direct and indirect free kicks, which will be dealt with later on, there are five other forms of restarts, or 'set pieces' as they are frequently known. One of them, the place kick or kick-off, has already been described and occurs at the start of each half and after a goal has been scored.

The next three consist of the throw-in, the goal kick and the corner kick. These are dealt with separately under Laws 15 to 17. The final one, the 'drop-ball', does not have a Law to itself.

● THE THROW-IN

It will be remembered that the longer lines bordering the pitch are known as the touchlines and when the whole of the ball passes over the whole of the touchline, either on the ground or in the air, there has to be a method of returning it into play. Originally the ball was kicked back but later a one-handed throw was adopted, as in a rugby line-out. Finally the Law was altered again to require two hands to be used when propelling the ball back into play.

FIFA has expressed the view that it would like to see kick-ins again replace throw-ins and has conducted a series of experiments on that practice, but it is the current principles of the Law that are recited here. The ball is returned into play from the point where it crossed the line, by a player from the opposing team to that which had put it out of play, whether by a hand in the case of a goalkeeper or the foot, head or any part of the anatomy other than the hands by a field player. The throw-in can be made in any

Vinny Jones, making his debut for Wales, launches a throw-in. Long throw-ins have become a major attacking ploy in the modern game. Linesmen must ensure the player observes the touchline when taking the throw.

direction. There are a number of requirements, the first of which is that the thrower, at the actual moment of delivering the ball with his hands, has to face the field of play and part of each of his feet must be either on the touchline itself or on the ground behind the touchline. However, in the latter case referees usually allow the ball to be thrown from no more than a yard or so behind the line since otherwise the ball will not necessarily be thrown in from the correct place directed by the Law. As the thrower has to use both hands he must deliver the ball from behind and over his head. Although players are often seen to throw the ball 'up the line', as it is sometimes referred to, such a throw technically is not a fair one because in practice the thrower is not actually facing the field of play but is, instead, parallel to it.

Once the ball passes back into the field it is in play but the thrower may not play the ball again until it has been touched or played by another player of either side. Although some players have achieved the distinction of being able to throw the ball from the touchline into the goal itself, which is no mean feat, a goal cannot be scored directly from a throw-in. If the ball is not touched by a defender following an attacker's throw-in and passes over the goal line either in the goal itself or over the goal line by the side of the goal the referee awards a goal kick. If the ball is touched by a defender before passing over the goal

line, but not inside the goal, the referee will award a corner. In the unusual event of a defender throwing the ball directly into his own goal or over the goal line by the side of his goal the referee will award a corner kick to the opposition, as he would if the throw touched or was played by a defender so that it passed over the goal line.

The throw-in is technical in its nature and can be performed incorrectly through either misuse of the hands or failure to keep part of each foot on the ground in the correct position. If a throw-in is performed incorrectly it is termed a 'foul throw'. If a foul throw occurs the throw-in is awarded to the opposing team. A particularly important type of foul throw is where the thrower attempts to 'steal' ground. If that happens the referee should immediately award the throw-in to the opposition from the point at which the ball initially left the field of play.

No opposing player is allowed to dance about or gesticulate in any way calculated to distract or impede the thrower. Opponents need not be 10 yds from thrower. but if they come so close that he cannot fully bend and extend his arms this in effect is obstructing the thrower. Although the object for the thrower is generally to find a team-mate with the ball, the thrower must not throw the ball into the back of one of his own players in order to obtain the rebound. Likewise the thrower may not deliberately throw the ball against any part of the body of an opponent in order similarly to gain the rebound.

The punishment for these and further infringements of the throw-in Law is discussed on pages 47–55.

● THE GOAL KICK

When it passes over the goal line, what happens depends on whether the ball was last touched by an attacker or a defender. If it was touched by a defender a corner kick results, but if it was last touched by an attacker the restart will be by a goal kick. It is necessary for the whole of the ball to pass over the goal line on the outside of the posts either in the air or on the ground before the referee signals a goal kick for the purposes of a restart. If, of course, the ball passes over the goal line between the goal posts, the result is a goal.

Let us assume that the ball has not passed into the goal and that a goal kick rather than a corner is to be taken. It may be kicked from either side of the goal, at the kicker's discretion, from any point within the goal area by any member of the defending team. (At one time the Law specified that the goal kick should be taken from the side on which the ball passed over the goal line. However, it was felt that in order to speed up the game it would be advantageous for the defending side to

be allowed to take their goal kick from any point within the goal area.) It is necessary for the ball to pass beyond the penalty area; if it fails to do so it is not 'in play'. If this provision is infringed the kick has to be retaken.

The kicker is not allowed to play the ball a second time until it has been touched or played by another player of either his or the opposing team. Whether it would be physically possible to score a goal direct from a goal kick is a matter of conjecture but is irrelevant because the Law does not allow a goal to be scored direct from such a kick.

Players from the defending side may be positioned inside the penalty area at the taking of a goal kick but players from the opposing team must remain outside of the penalty area until the ball itself has been kicked clear of the penalty area.

● THE CORNER KICK

If a defender plays the ball over the goal line, either intentionally or unintentionally (even by means of a deflection), a corner kick results. It matters not whether the ball crosses the line in the air or on the ground as long as the whole of the ball crosses the whole of the line. When that happens the referee awards a corner kick to be taken from the quarter circle at the corner flag nearest to the point at which the ball crossed the line. (When the rules concerning the goal kick were amended to allow it to be taken from either side of the goal the

corresponding rules for a corner kick remained unaltered.) If the ball goes out of play to the right of the goal the corner is taken from that side and correspondingly for the left side. The whole of the ball has to be placed within the appropriate quadrant or quarter circle and the flag-post must not be moved.

Note that a goal *may* be scored direct from a corner kick. The kicker is not allowed to play the ball a second time before it has been touched or played by another player of either team. At the taking of a corner the defending side must stand a minimum distance of 10 yds from the ball until it is in play, which occurs when it has moved the distance of its own circumference. Sometimes the kicker may indicate that the corner flag is in the way of his taking a certain kind of kick, particularly when he wants to take an in-swinging kick. That is unfortunate, but does not entitle him to remove the corner flag, which must at all times remain in position unless it is broken, in which case it has to be replaced. For all infringements other than the attacker playing the ball twice, the kick must be retaken. In the unusual event that from a legitimately taken kick the ball strikes a goal post and rebounds to the player who took the kick, he may not play the ball again because to do so would mean infringing the rule stating that the ball may not be played a second time by the same player before it has been touched by another player.

INFRINGEMENTS AND PUNISHMENTS

There are three types of punishment for misconduct:

1 an indirect free kick, from which a goal may be scored only if the ball touches either an attacker or a defender in its flight;
2 a direct free kick, from which a goal can be scored without another player touching or playing the ball; and
3 a penalty, which is in effect a direct free kick taken from the penalty mark or spot, for an offence of a serious nature which is committed in the penalty area.

The game is supposed to be played with the spirit of the Laws uppermost, but the letter of the Law has to be upheld. Laws 12, 13 and 14 all deal with fouls and misconduct of one sort or another.

A direct free kick will be awarded for any one of ten offences, nine of which are physical and one is technical. The nine infringements which are committed when a player commits one of the following offences against an opponent:

1 kicks or attempts to kick the opponent;
2 trips or throws him by use of any part of the body, or by stooping in front of or behind him;
3 jumps at him;
4 charges him in a careless or reckless manner; or charges him from behind unless the opponent is obstructing;
5 strikes or attempts to strike him;
6 spits at him;
7 holds him;
8 pushes him;
9 when tackling, makes contact with an opponent before making contact with the ball.

Many of the above offences can be treated by a referee as being so serious that the offender is either cautioned or, worse, dismissed from the field.

The tenth, technical offence for which a direct free kick is given is

deliberately handling the ball by either striking it or propelling it with hand or arm, whether it be the forearm or upper arm. Obviously this does not apply to the defending goalkeeper within his own penalty area but does apply to an attacking goalkeeper if he happens to appear in his opponent's penalty area.

The direct free kick is taken by the opposing team from the place where the offence occurred unless it was committed by an attacker in his opponent's goal area in which case the kick can be taken from any point within that goal area.

The above offences are often referred to as 'penal offences' because if they are committed by *a defender in his own penalty area* his team is punished by the award of a penalty kick against it. Such a penalty kick can be awarded irrespective of where the ball is at the time the incident occurred as long as the ball is in play. A defender who thus kicked an opponent while the ball was out by the touchline would still be guilty of a penal offence for which a penalty would be awarded.

When it comes to indirect free kicks the misconduct involved is many and various. Anything which can be considered to be 'ungentlemanly conduct' can lead to the award of an indirect free kick including technical

Definitely against the Laws! Alan Shearer is held back illegally by Gheorghe Popescu in an England v. Romania game.

offences and misdemeanours which although not serious are sufficient to warrant some form of punishment. Any of the following will cause an indirect free kick to be awarded:

1 Playing in a dangerous manner, which can include high kicking, showing studs to an opponent when going for the ball without intending to kick the opponent, ducking low to put an opponent into danger or even attempting to kick the ball while it is being held by the goalkeeper.

2 Charging an opponent fairly with the shoulder but when the ball is not within playing distance of either of the players concerned and while they are not trying to make contact with the ball.

3 Intentionally impeding an opponent's progress while not attempting to play the ball oneself. This is defined as interposing the body between the opponent and the ball as an obstacle to the opponent.

4 Charging the goalkeeper when he does not have both feet on the ground while he is holding the ball and has not passed outside the goal area. If a goalkeeper obstructs an opponent he is allowed to be charged.

5 If a player is guilty of any one of a number of actions which are intended to embarrass an opponent and are not within the letter or spirit of the Laws. These include leaning on the shoulders of another player of his own team in order to head the ball; entering or leaving the field of play without the permission of the referee no matter what the cause; intentionally stretching his arms up to impede an opponent at the taking of a throw-in or forcing an opponent to change course by the movement of arms up and down even though bodily contact is not made, or performing the same kind of ritual to obstruct the opposing goalkeeper and so prevent him from putting the ball back into play. In addition, an indirect free kick is awarded if a player causes an opponent to leave the ball by a trick or uses any form of trick in order to circumvent the Laws of the game, particularly one which is intended to overcome the goalkeeper's inability to receive the ball into his hands after it has been kicked to him deliberately by a team-mate.

6 There are also a number of offences punishable by an indirect free kick relating solely to the goalkeeper within his own penalty area. These are as follows:

a Taking more than four steps in any direction from the moment the goalkeeper takes control of the ball. Such control consists of holding, bouncing or throwing the ball in the air and then catching it again without actually releasing it into play.

b Having actually released the ball into play within the prescribed number of steps, touching it again with his hands before it has been touched or played by an opponent either inside or outside of his penalty area or by a player of his own team outside of the penalty area.

c Touching the ball with his hands after it has been deliberately kicked to him by a member of his own team. The team-mate is allowed to head, chest or use any other part of his body (apart from the hands or arms) to return the ball to the goalkeeper but he must not deliberately kick it with the foot.

d Indulging in tactics which in the opinion of the referee are intended to waste time by holding up the game, including intentionally lying on the ball longer than is necessary after a save has been made. In the latter case, the first offence is a caution and a repetition means a dismissal.

An indirect free kick is always awarded in those set piece or restart positions where the kicker plays the ball a second time before a player from either side has touched the ball. There is also provision for an indirect free kick to be awarded against a penalty taker who infringes the penalty kick regulations.

Finally, the infringement of offside is treated as a necessary stoppage in play and the attackers who have allowed themselves to become offside are punished for doing so by the award of an indirect free kick against them (although in this case the distinction between an indirect free kick and a direct one is purely technical).

There are a number of rules relating to the taking of free kicks of either variety. First, a player taking such a kick inside his own penalty area is entitled to require all opposing players to be 10 yds from the ball. They have to be outside the kicker's own penalty area and remain so until the ball has been kicked out of the area itself. In those circumstances the defending side may not play the ball to a colleague for him to kick it out of the area because if the ball is not kicked direct into play beyond the penalty area it is treated as a nullity and the kick has to be retaken.

When free kicks are taken from outside the penalty area again all opponents must be 10 yds from the ball. Where the free kick is indirect and is taken less than 10 yds from the defender's goal line they are allowed to be on their goal line between the goal posts.

Frequently when a direct free kick is awarded within shooting distance of the goal the defenders line up to form a 'defensive wall' and the kick is often termed a 'ceremonial' one. Once the attacking team has decided that it wants its opponents 10 yds back the referee must not allow the free kick to be taken until the defenders are ready. However, if the attackers do not want a ceremonial free kick they are entitled to take the kick when they are ready provided the referee signals that they may do so. The advantage therefore is always intended to be with the team that has had its player fouled.

With all free kicks the ball must be stationary and the kicker is not allowed to play the ball a second time until it has been touched or played by another player of either side.

The free kick itself must be taken as near to the point at which the foul occurred as possible, except that any free kick awarded to the defending team within its own goal area may be taken anywhere within that goal area and an indirect free kick awarded to the attacking team within its opponent's goal area must be taken from that part of the goal area line at the point nearest to where the foul was committed.

In order to signal for an indirect, as opposed to a direct, free kick the referee raises his arm above his head and keeps it there until the kick has been taken and the ball subsequently touched by a player from either side other than the kicker.

A particular point to note is that it is not possible for a defender to score an own goal from either a direct or indirect free kick. If from outside his own penalty area a defender kicks the ball into his goal the referee awards a corner kick. Another point is that at an indirect free kick, should the attacker taking the kick kick the ball directly into his opponents' goal, by definition no goal can be scored and a goal kick is awarded to the defenders.

● THE PENALTY KICK

A penalty kick is for more serious offences committed within a side's own penalty area. Taken from the penalty mark, it can be awarded irrespective of where the ball is at the time the offence is committed provided that the ball is in play at the time and the offence itself takes place in the penalty area. A goal can be scored directly from the kick or the ball may be passed forwards for an attacker to run on to from 10 yds behind the kicker and attempt to score. However, once the ball has rolled the distance of its circumference from the penalty spot, if a direct shot at goal is not made the opposing goalkeeper or defenders may also attempt to play the ball. At the moment when the kick is being taken all players (with the exception of the kicker, who has been identified to the opposing goalkeeper, and that goalkeeper himself) must be within the field of play but outside the penalty area itself and at least 10 yds behind the penalty spot.

The defending goalkeeper must stand on his own goal line and between the goal posts until the ball is kicked. He may move his body but may not move his feet until the ball has been struck. Although, as indicated, the kicker must play the ball forwards he may not touch the ball a second time until it has been touched or played by a team-mate or opponent.

If either team infringes these regulations one of three things can happen. First, an infringement by the defending team will mean that the kick is retaken if a goal has *not* been scored. Second, an infringement by the attacking team will cause the goal, if one has been scored, to be disallowed. In those circumstances the kick is again retaken. However, if the kicker infringes, an indirect free kick will be given against him from the point at which the infringement occurred but subject to the various other provisions of the Laws which may supervene. Third, in the event of interference by an outside agency, such as spectators, the kick will be retaken unless the ball has rebounded into play from the goalkeeper, the bar or a post and is *then* stopped by an outside agency. If that occurs the referee must restart the game by dropping the ball at the appropriate place.

Examples of infringements which require the retaking of a penalty kick are as follows:

1 Where the kick is missed but the goalkeeper has not taken up position on the goal line or has moved his feet before the kick is taken or there is encroachment by the defending side at the time of taking the kick.

2 Where the goal is scored but there is encroachment by the attacking side or the kicker is guilty of ungentlemanly conduct.

3 Where the kick is taken, whether or not a goal is scored, and there is encroachment by *both* sides.

A match must be extended at half-time or full-time to allow the penalty kick to be taken or retaken as the case may be, but the extension lasts only until the moment that the kick has been completed, which occurs when a goal has been scored, a save made or the penalty missed. In these circumstances a missed penalty occurs not only if the ball is struck wide of the goal altogether, but also if it hits a post or the crossbar and rebounds out.

There are numerous procedures and checklists relating to the taking of penalty kicks where the teams are on level terms at the end of cup competitions and the fixture has to be decided by what has been commonly termed a 'penalty shoot-out'. A shoot-out is not considered to be part of the match but of course is the deciding factor as to who wins the competition or proceeds to the next round. Initially there are up to five such kicks with the winner being the team that scores the highest aggregate. If the teams are level after five penalty kicks each then 'sudden death' applies: when one team scores and its opponents miss that is the end of the penalty decider.

Tomas Brolin of Sweden is successful with his penalty kick against Germany in the semi-final of the European Championships. The keeper must not move until the ball is kicked and the referee should insist on the kick being retaken if he moves too early and gains an advantage by doing so.

THE PUNISHMENTS FOR SERIOUS MISCONDUCT

Indirect free kicks, direct free kicks and penalties may in many instances be sufficient to punish the offender. However, in certain instances a player will infringe in such a way that for the good of the player, his team, his opponents or indeed the game itself that player has to be more severely punished. To cover that, the football law makers have provided the referee with certain sanctions which enable him to carry out his duties more effectively within the spirit and letter of the Laws.

Thus a player is to be cautioned and shown a yellow card if he is guilty of any of the following:

1 During the course of the match, leaving the field (except through accident) or entering or re-entering the game without the referee's permission *and* signal.
2 Persistent infringement of the Laws.
3 Showing dissent to a referee's (and in some cases a linesman's) decision, by word or action, unless it be in such an excessive manner as to require more serious action on the part of the referee.
4 Tackling an opponent either by a lateral sliding tackle or from behind, if the player making the tackle instead of making contact with the ball trips his opponent.
5 Ungentlemanly conduct, which is defined according either to the letter of the Law or to its overriding spirit. Ungentlemanly conduct encompasses specifically any of the following, although the list is not exhaustive:
   a Leaning on a colleague's shoulders to head the ball: or throwing the ball against the back of a colleague to receive the rebound.
   b The intentional use of the arms *or* body to impede an opponent, especially the opposition goalkeeper, in order to delay the playing of the ball, rather than

The sliding tackle must be perfectly timed to be judged fair by the referee. Stuart Pearce's tackle on Flemming Poulsen of Denmark has intercepted the ball and appears entirely correct.

mere obstruction by interposition of the body between opponent and the ball.

c On the part of the goalkeeper, lying on the ball longer than is necessary, in the referee's opinion, after making a save.

d On the part of a defender, using a deliberate trick to overcome the rule by which defenders are prevented from kicking the ball intentionally to the goalkeeper for the latter to handle it. It is irrelevant whether or not the goalkeeper subsequently touches the ball with his hand or hands. Note that it is the defender, *not* the goalkeeper, who is penalized and cautioned for this.

e Time wasting (in the opinion of the referee).

In each of these circumstances the game is restarted by an indirect free kick unless a more serious breach of the Laws has occurred. The referee is not obliged to stop the game if he sees an offence which he wishes to caution; he may instead implement the advantage clause and let the non-offending team play on. If he does so he must, however, caution the guilty player when the ball next goes 'dead' (i.e. is no longer in play).

Although a caution is considered sufficient in the circumstances previously referred to, in some situations either repetition of the offence or the perpetration of a more grave offence will lead to a player being dismissed from the field. There is a distinction between a repetition of a less serious offence, in which case a second yellow card is shown followed by a red card, and a grave offence in which case simply the red card is shown prior to dismissal.

Thus a player is sent off with both cards being shown when he is guilty of a second cautionable offence after having received an initial caution, or where the referee is about to caution a

Yellow and red cards for cautions and sendings-off were introduced into the senior game to avoid confusion over language difficulties. This picture shows Paul Gascoigne receiving a booking in the World Cup semi-final in 1990 which meant he would have missed the final even if England had won this game (in fact, they lost it on penalties).

player and before he has had an opportunity to do so the player commits another offence which merits a caution. The circumstances in which the red card only are shown relate to:

1 A player guilty of using foul or abusive language.
2 A player guilty of violent conduct, which incorporates striking, attempting to strike or spitting at an opponent, a colleague or the officials.
3 A player is guilty of serious foul play. This covers the following situations (the list is not exhaustive):
  a A player tackles from behind violently and with little or no attempt to play the ball.
  b Where a player moving towards his opponents' goal with an obvious goal-scoring opportunity is, in the opinion of the referee, intentionally impeded by an opponent by any kind of unlawful

means, thus denying the attacking player's team the chance to score a goal. This also applies when a defending goalkeeper pulls down an opponent in that situation.
  c A player (other than the goalkeeper in his own penalty area) denies his opponents a goal or an obvious goal-scoring opportunity by intentionally handling the ball. Thus if a defender punches the ball off the goal line or, being outside the penalty area, handles the ball to stop such a goal-scoring opportunity he will be dismissed. This also applies to the goalkeeper handling the ball outside his penalty area to stop such an opportunity, since once out of his penalty area the goalkeeper is subject to the same rules as any other player. In this instance it is up to the referee to decide whether the goalkeeper is merely guilty of ungentlemanly conduct or is in fact attempting to stop his opponents from scoring a goal.

The subsequent free kick to restart the game should not be taken until the dismissed player has left the field. In the event of two players being dismissed at the same time, it is a sensible practice for the referee and the nearest linesman to escort off one player each, thus avoiding any further confrontations.

THE OFFICIALS

There are three types of official who control football at senior level. They are, first, a referee; second, two linesmen; and third, a 'fourth official' so designated. Each of these officials is considered in turn, in order of their importance. (In very junior football linesmen may be dispensed with where it is not possible to obtain them but a game cannot be played without a referee.)

● THE REFEREE

Although numbers of players can be reduced, goal nets can be dispensed with and various other minor modifications to the game can take place, arguably the referee is the most important factor of all since no match can take place without him (or, increasingly, her). The referee is the sole arbiter of both the written Laws and the 'spirit' of the game. The referee's authority and his right to enforce the Laws commence as soon as he enters the field of play and continue until he leaves the ground on which the match is played.

While the 17 Laws and the various rulings exist in written form, the referee has at all times to administer those Laws as he feels appropriate. This is especially so where the Law dictates that a decision shall be made according to 'the referee's opinion'. How then does the referee interpret his discretion as distinct from mandatory provisions laid down? Stanley Lover, a leading writer on refereeing topics and a noted FIFA lecturer, advocates three basic principles. These are *equality* – those who take part in the game must have an equal opportunity to demonstrate individual skills; *safety* – the health of the players must be safeguarded in normal match play; and *enjoyment* – the game should provide the maximum pleasure for all who take part.

Thus the referee has the power to penalize throughout the period of active play or indeed when play has been temporarily suspended or where the ball has gone dead for any reason, such as when it is out of play. Where he considers it appropriate he can refrain from penalizing in cases where he is satisfied that by so refraining it will in turn give an advantage to the attacking team.

Even if the referee makes a mistake his decision on points of fact concerning the play itself is final so far as the result of the game is concerned. Thus it is almost impossible for a match to be replayed on the grounds of a basic mistake by a referee during the course of play. There have been numerous examples of such incidents. One of the most famous of which occurred when Huddersfield Town were relegated after a match with Tottenham Hotspur where a Spurs player struck a corner kick against the referee, collected the rebound and centred for one of his team-mates to score. Although the corner kicker should have been penalized for playing the ball twice the goal stood and the match was not replayed. Another refereeing mistake occurred when Maradona of Argentina punched the ball into the England net during a World Cup international match in 1986. The goal was allowed to stand and so was the result.

Apart from enforcing the Laws the referee also has a number of administrative duties. He must therefore keep a record of the game and act as the timekeeper, which means allowing the full or agreed time plus all time lost through accident or other cause. Those other causes can and should include transporting injured players from the field, time wasting and a multitude of other problems including invasions of the pitch by humans or animals or adverse weather conditions. It also includes a provision for adding the time utilized in substituting players. A general rule of thumb is that a substitution takes approximately 30 seconds, so the referee should calculate the number of substitutions during each half of a game and add on the appropriate amount of time at the end of that half. Finally, the referee must satisfy himself that the ball provided for the match meets with the appropriate requirements.

The referee has a number of discretionary powers. He can stop the game for any infringement of the Laws, or suspend or even terminate it whenever he considers a stoppage to be necessary because of such things as interference by spectators or serious adverse or inclement weather conditions. In those cases the referee has a duty to submit a detailed report to the competent authority regulating the competition under whose jurisdiction the match was played.

Also coming under his discretion is the right to stop the game if he feels a player has been seriously injured, but

Paul Ince of Manchester United and Robbie
Slater of Blackburn tangle in a typical one-on-
one challenge which the referee will have to
interpret dozens of times in every game.

he should then attempt to have the player removed as soon as possible from the field with the intention of immediately resuming the game. In order to discourage players from feigning injury there has been a recent tightening up of the clauses in Law 5 that give the referee his powers and jurisdiction. If a player is slightly injured the game is not stopped until the ball has 'gone dead'. The referee, who has sole discretion, generally allows no person other than the players and linesmen to enter the field without his permission but is now required to call on the medical assistant in charge of the injured player's team to examine the injured player and to organize his removal from the field. The only exception to this ruling is in the case of an obviously serious injury and/or where a head injury occurs. The International Board, mindful of the welfare of players, has recommended to referees the need for a rapid assessment in these circumstances. Care is the paramount consideration for the seriously injured player and referees are encouraged to err on the side of safety and accept the advice of a team's medical adviser, be he the trainer, physiotherapist or club doctor.

Arguably the most important of the referee's functions is to control the game by means of administering punishments. The referee must stop the game for any infringement of the Laws that involve fouls and misconduct. Where the infringement is a flagrant breach of the Laws the referee is required to caution and show a yellow card to any guilty player. For both flagrant and serious breaches of the Laws the referee must show a red card and send off the field of play any player who in his opinion has been guilty of violent conduct, serious foul play, the use of foul or abusive language or one who persists in misconduct after having received a caution. If a player commits two infringements of a different nature at the same time the referee punishes the more serious offence. This is important for the displaying of the appropriate coloured card. After some considerable confusion as to whether the card should be shown first and the caution administered second or whether the caution should precede the showing of the card it has been finally decided by the International Board that the appropriately coloured card should be shown first. Thus when cautioning a player the referee produces a yellow card and then enquires the name of the offender and delivers a caution, explaining which offence the player has committed. The referee also notifies the player that if he persists in misconduct after having received the caution he will be dismissed from the field. If a player commits a sending-off offence and is expelled from the field the referee follows the same procedure as for a caution save that he will produce a single red card. If, on the other hand, a player already cautioned commits a second cautionable offence in the match the referee will then be required to dismiss the player but in this instance must show first the yellow card and immediately after it the red card. This is to make it obvious that the player is being sent off for a second cautionable offence and not for a single red-card offence. When the ruling was first introduced the referee was required to produce both the red and yellow cards in the same hand at the same time. This, however, proved to be impractical for a number of reasons, hence the alteration in the ruling.

At the time of the cautioning or sending off, the referee must make a note of the player's name (sometimes also the number on the back of his shirt if there is likely to be some confusion), the time of the offence, the name of the player's team and the reason for the caution or dismissal. Within the prescribed period of time laid down by the competition concerned the referee is required to send the name of the offender and the reason for the caution or dismissal to the competent authority, whose disciplinary committee will deal with that offender. The referee is also required to submit misconduct reports to the competent authority regarding misconduct by club officials or any other breach of the Laws or rules of the competition which come to his notice. These include matters which may affect the field of play, the ball, the conduct of spectators or anything else which interferes with the control of the match by him and his linesmen.

The referee has power to produce the yellow or red card only for 'on-field' misconduct. In the case of misconduct by trainers, managers, coaches or other club officials, he may require them to leave the environs of the pitch. It is prudence rather than decree advocates that a player who is dismissed from the field of play should not be allowed to return to the side of the pitch during the remainder of the game.

The referee's further duties include signalling for a number of aspects of the match, including the commencement of play at the start of each half, which must be by use of his whistle. (For all other restarts a hand signal may suffice.) The official signals reproduced in this book (starting overleaf) are those for an indirect free kick, a corner, a goal kick and the implementation of the advantage clause. Where a free kick is awarded the referee must give the appropriate directional signal.

The referee may not allow any person to enter the field of play until play has stopped or until he has given him the signal to do so, but sometimes the referee will authorize his linesmen to take certain active steps. The referee should not accept the intervention of a linesman if he himself has seen the incident from his position on the field and is better able to judge that incident. It is the duty of the referee to act upon information of neutral linesmen in cases where an incident has not come to the referee's

Official signals by the referee

Play on – advantage
Where the referee sees an offence but uses the advantage rule, he indicates that play should continue.

Caution or expulsion
A yellow card indicates a cautionary booking. A player committing a second bookable offence is shown another yellow card, followed by a red card and is sent off. A lone red card is shown for the most serious offences.

Indirect free kick
This signal is maintained until the kick has been taken and retained until the ball has been played or touched by another player or goes out of play.

Direct free kick
The hand and arm clearly indicate the direction.

Penalty kick
The referee clearly indicates the penalty mark, but there is no need for him to run towards it.

Goal kick

Corner kick

attention. If, for example, a linesman indicates that he has seen something upon which the referee is prepared to act the referee can reverse his first decision so long as he has not restarted the game.

Where a referee decides to apply the advantage clause he cannot reverse that decision if the advantage does not materialize, even though he has not given the signal indicating that the advantage clause is being applied. If a referee allows an advantage he is still required to deal with the offence after play has stopped, if it is sufficiently serious. In that event the referee should return to the offending player and either caution or dismiss him according to the seriousness of the offence committed.

Unless he has a photographic memory it is unlikely that a referee will be able to remember every incident which takes place and which he is required to record. As a result the match official will take on to the field of play with him various aids to record what takes place. These will include writing materials, including preferably a notebook or record cards (which are now pre-prepared for referees, printed with numbers of recurring items to register) and preferably a pencil (rather than a ballpoint or other ink writer which can smudge in wet weather or even fail to write at all on wet paper), plus possibly spares of both of these items. In order for the referee to fulful his function as timekeeper he must carry or wear a stop-watch. (Some referees both wear a stop-watch on their wrist and carry a pocket watch in their uniform.) To control play a whistle is mandatory and the referee should always ensure that either he or one of his linesmen carry a spare whistle in case of emergency. One or more coins should also be taken on to the field to be spun at the start of the match in order to decide kick-off or choice of ends. Finally, in senior matches the referee will also take the match ball on to the pitch while one of the linesmen will carry on a spare ball.

It is the duty of the referee to designate which of his linesmen shall be the senior linesman and the one who takes over from him in case of emergency; to give various instructions with regard to the control and running of the game, especially in relation to offsides; and to deal with all other matters of co-operation between the three of them.

It is essential for the referee and linesmen to be clearly visible and readily distinguished from all other persons on the field of play. Referees are thus required to wear a uniform, something that in recent years has proved to be troublesome. Originally the referee wore a blazer and plus-fours normally in the colours of the organization he represented, be it school, club or university. As time progressed the blazer gave way to an army-style tunic top. Finally, during the early 1950s came the black top with the white trimmings, the credit for

pioneering which is ascribed to Ken Aston. For three decades the black jersey with white trimmings or all-black jersey coupled with black shorts and black socks with or without white tops was the accepted referees' uniform. The only exception was in international matches involving Scotland, who wore navy blue shirts which through tradition they were allowed to retain. Recently, with more colourful combinations being utilized by players and especially goalkeepers, experiments have taken place with referees' kits. As a result, in England the Premier League referees have worn green for the past few seasons. Football League referees were initially allowed to wear purple or yellow as a variation on black, but this experiment has now been discontinued. In the 1994 World Cup finals in the USA, referees were offered the choice of three colours (red, yellow or grey), which has been retained subsequently, but it is unclear where these experiments will ultimately lead. Whatever the combination, the position still remains that the referee must at all times be distinguished and distinguishable, by the colours he wears, from the contesting teams.

In domestic competitions the referees are drawn from the ranks of the national list but in international matches they must be selected from a neutral country and from a panel maintained by FIFA unless the countries concerned agree to appoint their own officials.

Attempts are being made to limit the legal liability for injury or damage to players, officials or spectators resulting from referees' decisions but these must be considered in the light of each country's legal system.

● THE LINESMEN

The position of linesmen is somewhat unusual in that in all senior football and in much junior football, a linesman is already a qualified referee. His duties as specified by Law 6 are somewhat sparsely defined. Thus two linesmen are appointed to each game and, subject to anything the referee may decide upon, their duties consist of (a) determining when the ball is in or out of play; (b) indicating, when the ball goes out of play, whether it has gone out for a corner kick, a goal kick or a throw-in; and (c) indicating to the referee when one or both sides wish to make a substitution.

Most surprisingly, there is actually nothing in the Law to specify that the linesmen shall indicate to the referee when an offside has occurred. This strange omission is remedied by references to a written memorandum of co-operation between the referee and the linesmen and by the referee's directions to the linesmen prior to the commencement of the game. Otherwise the linesmen's obligations consist of generally assisting the referee to control the game in accordance with the Laws.

Signals by linesmen fall into two categories: official and unofficial. Official signals are always given by the use of the flag supplied to the linesmen either by the club (in senior football) or by the referee (in junior football). Unofficial signals tend to correspond with those hand signals which the referee would give officially during the course of the match. Thus the unofficial signals are a code or language between the referee on the pitch and the linesmen on the sidelines. However, linesmen's unofficial signals should in general be discouraged.

It is particularly important that linesmen who see an offence or breach of the Laws commited bring it to the referee's attention if the referee has not seen it. Where, however, the referee has seen the incident the linesmen should not attempt to interfere but should allow the referee to run the game in his own fashion. Furthermore, there are occasions where a linesman justifiably flags for an incident but the referee decides to implement the advantage clause and 'play on', in which event he will signal to the linesman that he has seen his flag and that the linesman should now lower it.

At international level the linesmen's flags must be of a sufficiently vivid colour to attract the referee's attention against the background of the crowd. They are now generally either bright red or yellow or a combination of red and yellow squares. Many national competitions suggest that one linesman should have a plain-coloured flag and the other a flag containing squares.

Linesmen are usually appointed by their country's national association, but those in international matches are expected to be of a neutral nationality.

A further important function of the linesmen comes at the taking of a penalty kick, when the referee will instruct one linesman either to act as a goal judge to see whether the ball crosses the line or (if the referee himself takes up position on the goal line) to guard against encroachment.

Official signals by the linesman

Offside
Flag held upright to indicate offside.

Offside
Position on the near side of the field.

Offside
When the referee stops play, the linesman indicates position on the far side of the field.

Offside
Position near the centre of the field.

Throw-in
Note this is a directional signal.

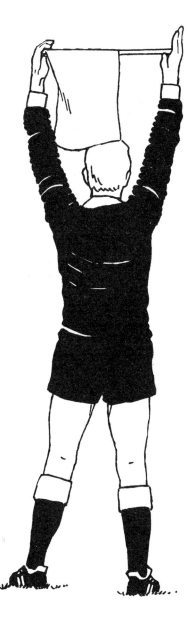 

Back view
Linesman signalling to the referee for a substitution to be made.

Front view
Linesman signalling to the referee when a substitute is waiting at the halfway line.

Goal kick

Corner kick

The linesman may first need to signal that the ball has gone out of play if there is any doubt. He should also look at the referee in case the latter has already made his own decision, which may be different from the linesman's.

THE FOURTH OFFICIAL

For many years, referees and linesmen would go in trepidition of an injury occurring, to one of their number. If that happened during the match and one of them had to leave the field without any possibility of returning, there would obviously be a void and at senior level the possibility of the game having to be abandoned. The alternative was to summon up anyone, be it a spectator or club official, who was a qualified referee to act as a substitute linesman (if the referee was injured the senior linesman always took over the refereeing duties).

Many associations, particularly the English Football League, worried by the number of times this type of incident was occurring, decided that they would prefer to have a 'fourth qualified official' available at all their matches. This idea has now been implemented by FIFA. In senior football only the highest-class referee can be a fourth official and at international level only a referee or linesman appointed to the international panel may so officiate.

There is now written into the guidelines a formal role for the fourth official, which consists of officiating as either referee or linesman as the case may be, should the need arise. His other duties off the field include assisting with any other administrative matter before, during and after the match as required by the referee; assisting with substitution procedures during the match; and the control of replacement footballs where required. This avoids the referee having to test a fresh ball and keeps the time delay to a minimum. Finally, he has the authority to check the equipment of substitutes before they enter the field of play and if all is not correct he tells one of the linesmen who in turn informs the referee.

It is important to remember that the fourth official has only limited status within the Laws of the game; that is, that there is no reference to him in the 17 Laws themselves. However, he has been given the duties described above, all of which are intended to assist the referee and his colleagues. It is an indication of how important this function is becoming that there were for the first time four officials appointed to each game in the 1994 World Cup, held in the USA.

ADMINISTRATING THE MATCH

Most national associations have a memorandum relating to co-operation between referees and linesmen. While there are no instructions relating to the positioning of the referee and linesman during the game, most referees in modern football adopt what is known as the 'diagonal system of control'. This involves the referee taking up position at the start of the game in an advance position in or just in front of the centre circle and being the focal point of an imaginary diagonal line running from corner to corner. The referee will choose whether he prefers his linesmen to run the 'right diagonal' or 'left diagonal', and stick approximately to the other diagonal himself. Whichever, he chooses, the linesmen will take up a position on the referee's right or left as the case may be and will always be in a position to face him and face each other. The referee will tend to move between the two positions as the linesmen move up and down one half of the pitch throughout the game. As football has become faster and more crowded in midfield the referee sometimes adopts a more double Z-like approach, thereby widening the diagonal run across the field and back the other way in the opposite half.

At substitutions the linesman nearest the point of the substitution is required to attract the attention of the referee by raising his flag above his head – the authorized signal. At goal kicks and at corner kicks the referee and linesmen decide where the linesmen will stand. Many linesmen stand behind the corner flag when the corner kick is on their side. A similar situation occurs at penalty kicks when the referee must notify the linesmen where they shall stand and their duties in relation to encroachment or being goal judge. The referee will further indicate how to deal with foul throws, the normal practice being that the linesman will watch for foot faults while the referee deals with technical hand faults.

Finally, as the referee has the sole control, he has the right to overrule the linesman and will show by a hand signal that he has done so. It has been suggested that linesmen be prompted to remember that they are 'assistants', not 'insistents'.

It is important to note the referee's various signals, including that for playing on in cases where he has decided to implement the advantage clause; and where he raises his arm above his head at the taking of an indirect free kick, to differentiate it from a direct free kick. The linesman will signal offside by waving the flag initially and then lowering it to one of three points to show whether the offside position was on the far side, the middle or near side of his area of play. The linesman will also indicate the direction of the throw-in but will make no signal at the scoring of a goal unless he has seen an infringement, whereupon he should stand his ground and bring the infringement to the referee's attention by waving his flag.

INDEX

Page numbers in **bold** refer to the illustrations